the one that came
after

ZA

BookLeaf Publishing

Presentation by *BookLeaf Publishing*

Web: www.bookleafpub.com

E-mail: info@bookleafpub.com

ISBN: 9789357213899

First edition 2023

for him

1.

"kiss me"
she said to him
as she leaned against the tree
with the crimson leaves
underneath the pink sky
not a cloud in sight
raindrops dancing around them.
"I want to remember this moment"
he smiled at her
the way only he could
and as he held her
his lips brushing against hers
she closed her eyes and prayed
that he would remember it too

2.

she rebuilt this house with her own hands
through sweat and splinters
turned ashes into a foundation
wreckage into walls
rubble into a roof

she has a home
and yet she finds herself
standing outside of his
filled with both faith and fear
asking him to let her in

- "please don't turn me away"

3.

sit with me
lay out your broken pieces
and I'll lay out mine
we can hurt each other with the sharp edges
or piece them together to create
something new
something beautiful
something whole

- what will it be?

4.

I have a fire to keep me warm
but I yearn for the warmth of yours
I have a place to lay my head
but I wonder what rest feels like
when I'm laying by your side
I have an entire table to myself
but I'd leave it to sit at yours

if you'll have me
so have me

5.

he's forgetful
and I don't mind it.
I don't care if he forgets my favorite color
he doesn't have to remember my coffee order
hell, even my birthday.
but sometimes I wonder
when we're apart
will he remember
the night he told me he loved me?
will he remember
what it tastes like when our tongues melt into
each other?
will he remember
that he said I was everything he prayed for?
will he remember
that I would have one more for him?
will he remember
the way that every moment we spend together
feels like home?
he's forgetful,
but I hope he'll remember that
because I can't forget it.

6.

"I'm listening"
and she knew he was
even though her words were like streams
that flowed into rivers
into lakes and gulfs and oceans
and back again
he was listening.

7.

O Uniter,
the one who brings together
Hydrogen and Oxygen
land and sky
bee and flower
unite me with my love
let him be the coolness of my eyes
and I, his.

8.

there was a time
when I was certain he was mine
and yet nights like tonight
I can feel him slipping through my fingertips
like little grains of sand
and all I can do
is let go

You can take my time
my heart
my thoughts
my hopes
my present
my future

but
love you as I may
I won't let you take
me for granted

10.

I used to pity myself
and thought of myself a fool
for how freely I gave my love away
pieces of my heart
scattered all over
left in the hands of
those who didn't know how to treat it.
but I've learned that I am not the one
who should be pitied
and that the foolish one
is he would once had a home
in the garden that beats in my chest
and now only holds a mere fragment of it
a leaf
a flake
a souvenir
a reminder
of the greatest love they will ever know
of what they will spend the rest of their lives
searching for in others
but there is no garden like mine.

11.

I've never seen someone fear love
just as deeply as they want it
I knew he was afraid
but I was willing to hold his hand
to stand by his side
as he fought his demons
to show him it didn't have to hurt
and for some time, he let me
and we walked through his darkness
until he couldn't anymore
he left me there to fend for myself
but I made it out
I just used the love and light I tried to give him
to guide me

12.

perhaps I am only meant
to love him like the moon
no matter how much I long for it
it can't meet me where I am
I could try to reach it
but I could hurt myself
with no guarantee of getting there
so I'll admire it here, from afar
and wish it well
my moon
my love

13.

"it's a new day," he said
and it was
the sun burned brighter
the birds harmonized louder
my cheeks almost hurt
from the smile spread across my face
love was real
and it was here
my second chance

14.

I pray he's written for me
and if he's not
I pray that He rewrites my story

15.

I don't expect you to fix me
just hold my hand
while I fix myself
be patient while my wounds heal
then kiss my scars
and tell me they're beautiful

16.

he said I'm like the sun
burning myself
to light the lives of others
and he was like the rain
but his clouds never dimmed my shine
they cradled it
and his showers brought a coolness
that was gentle
purifying
and only made my light
shine brighter

17.

I want to walk beside you
pray behind you
and love you for as long as I have in this life
then forever in the next

18.

sometimes it hurts so much
that I would rather have never felt love at all
than have it dangled in front of me
only for it to leave
as quickly as it arrived

19.

pain recognizes pain
and I saw his
and wanted to badly
to share it with him
to help him carry the load
but he chose his pain
over me
so now I'm left
carrying my own
only now
it's so much heavier

20.

I soaked my prayer mat in tears
thanking God for giving me
exactly what I had been waiting for
what I thought would never come
then I did it again
begging Him to help heal me
every time you walked away

21.

then one day I realized
the problem was that
I saw everything we could be
and he only saw everything we couldn't.
but I would give up my sight completely
just so he could see things through my eyes.

www.ingramcontent.com/pod-product-compliance
Lightning Source LLC
LaVergne TN
LVHW050309200726

843509LV00015B/3232